INDIANS

OF THE

LONGHOUSE

INDIANS

OF THE LONGHOUSE

THE STORY OF THE IROQUOIS

By SONIA BLEEKER

Illustrated by Althea Karr

NEW YORK

WILLIAM MORROW & COMPANY

1950

970.3
B

Thanks are due to Dr. William N. Fenton, Bureau of American Ethnology, Smithsonian Institution, Washington. D. C., for reading and criticizing the manuscript.

Fifteenth Printing, October, 1971

CONTENTS

Chapter

1

The Iroquois

FIVE HUNDRED years ago, before any European
explorer had set foot on the continent of North
America, Indian tribes lived in the hills and valleys of what is now central New York State. It
is hard to imagine how the country south of the
Adirondacks along the Hudson and Mohawk
rivers looked in those days. There were no towns

and cities, no boats on the rivers and lakes, except once in a while an Indian canoe. The farms and orchards that now line these valleys did not exist. Thick forests covered the land down to the banks of the rivers. But there were villages in this fertile country, at least twenty of them, and in them lived the Iroquois (E-ro-kwoy) Indians.

If you had entered one of these villages, you would have seen a dozen or so longhouses, large buildings looking for all the world like poorly made barns. These clustered around an open square in the center of the village. About fifty people lived in each longhouse and several hundred in each of the large villages.

Each Iroquois village was surrounded by a high wall or palisade of logs, driven into the ground side by side and tied near the top. A deep trench often was dug around this wall of logs on the outside. The single entrance through the palisade was closely guarded. Iroquois villages were usually built on hilltops or on high land between the forks of a river. That made it hard for any

stranger or any enemy to get into the village without being seen.

An Iroquois village was a noisy untidy place, muddy in spring and fall, dusty in summer. When the weather was warm, children and dogs overran the paths and open spaces. Men and women sat working at their different tasks in the shade of the longhouses. People walked back and forth through the village and out the single gateway to the cornfields, which lay below near the river, and to the river itself. The Iroquois had no wells. Some villages had springs, but more often the people carried their water up from the river.

These Iroquois, who called themselves "People of the Longhouse," did not dress or even look much like the Indians in picture books. They were well-built people of medium height. The men were rather thin, but strong and muscular. The women were often stouter, but they were muscular too, for they worked hard. The Iroquois were brown-eyed and they had straight black hair. Their skin was a light brown, like that of a per-

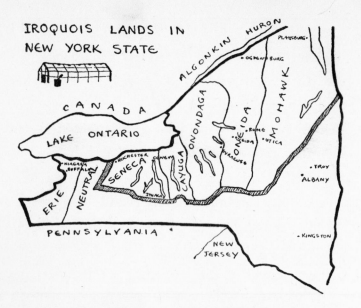

IROQUOIS LANDS IN NEW YORK STATE

son with a good coat of tan. Dressed in modern clothes, an Iroquois would scarcely be noticed in a crowd, though his cheekbones would be more prominent than ours.

The Iroquois Indians included five different tribes: Mohawk, Oneida, Onondaga, Cayuga, and Seneca. A sixth tribe was added later. The lands of the Mohawk lay nearest the Hudson River. The lands of the other four tribes were farther west.

According to Iroquois legends, the five tribes

had not always lived in central New York. In
the distant past their homes had been farther
to the north and east. Gradually moving into
this territory, they liked the fertile well-watered
land they found. The soil was rich and the forests
were full of deer, elk, moose, and bear. But this
new land was occupied by small bands of Algonkin
Indian hunters. It was only after a long series of
skirmishes and battles that the Iroquois tribes
gained control of the land they wanted.

As these five tribes spread through the valleys,
they often entered each other's territory and
fought among themselves—village against village. After many bloody raids and battles, they
became so weak that they could scarcely hold
their own against their common enemies, the
Algonkins. So, about 1570, the five tribes put an
end to their fighting with each other. The chiefs
met on the shores of Lake Onondaga and formed
the League of the Five Nations or the League of
the Iroquois. The story of how the League was
formed is told in Iroquois legends. An Onondaga,

named Hiawatha, first thought of uniting the warring tribes. He traveled through forests and by rivers to meet the chiefs of the different tribes and at last persuaded them all. They agreed to live in peace, to share their hunting grounds, and to fight together against their enemies. A Council, made up of chiefs of the five tribes, would make decisions for them. The Council would set the boundaries for each tribe's lands, but each tribe would choose the place where villages were to be built.

The Iroquois thus became an important power. Unlike many other Indian tribes, the Iroquois were farmers as well as hunters. Land was important to them, for the soil supplied their livelihood. They ate wild fruits, berries, and nuts. In the forests they found medicinal plants. Wood and bark from the trees were used to build houses and canoes, to make baskets, dishes, and many other things. Even more important were the plants the Iroquois cultivated. No one knows how or when these Indians or their ancestors first obtained corn.

By the time they came to New York, they were very dependent on the "three sisters" they brought with them—corn, beans, and squash.

The first and most important task when the Iroquois settled in new territory was clearing the land for farming. Forests of oak, maples, elms, and hickory covered most of the land. Evergreens grew in the colder, more mountainous parts. Even where the forest was thin, clearing the woods was hard work—harder for the Iroquois than for our pioneer forefathers. Our ancestors had axes, saws, plows, and the help of oxen and horses. The Iroquois farmers did not have these tools and animals. They did not have any iron or steel till after 1600. A short-handled stone hatchet was their only tool for cutting timber. For digging and cultivating the cleared land, they used digging sticks that looked like crude wooden shovels, and very crude hoes. The hoes were often made of a large shell tied to a stick.

Each man did not work his own fields, as our forefathers usually did. The Iroquois always worked together. Groups of families—sometimes as many as a hundred men, women, and children—labored together to fell the trees. The year before land was cleared, the men went out with their stone hatchets and cut through the bark all around the trunks of the trees they wanted to chop down. The sap could not flow through the girdled trunks and the trees began to die. Early the following spring they were cut down.

Cutting trees was long and slow work. First fires were built around the bases. To start a fire, a boy might bring some glowing embers from a

longhouse fire in a piece of bark. Or a fire might be made with a fire drill. When objects are rubbed together, heat is produced. The Iroquois used a fire drill made of a small stick of hard wood, which was spun round and round by a bow or by an up-and-down pumping action. The tip of the drill rested in a grooved piece of soft wood. Underneath this the Indians placed a small pile of dry shredded cornhusks, dried moss, or other tinder. As one man spun the stick, another blew the spark into a flame. In later years, when the Iroquois got steel from traders, they made fire with flint and steel, as did all the colonists at that time.

After the tree trunk had burned a little, the men chipped away the charred wood with their hatchets. The women slapped rings of clay and mud around the trunk, a few feet above the ground. That was to prevent the flames from spreading too high and spoiling the log. The burning and chipping continued day after day. After the trees had fallen and the branches had been chopped off, the logs were hauled to the village and used for building. Thus, little by little, the land was cleared to make room for the cornfields.

After the villagers had cleared the land, plots were set aside for each family to cultivate. All the crops a family grew belonged to that family. Actually, the crops belonged to the women of the family, who planted the seed and worked the fields. In times of need families shared their food, so no one went hungry. Often one village sent corn and beans to a neighboring village where the crops had failed or had been destroyed by an enemy.

Even after the land had been cleared, it looked nothing like a modern farm. There were no smooth, turned furrows. The charred stumps of trees stood like sentinels amid the rows of young corn. It took several hundred acres to feed a village, and the backbreaking job of clearing the land was never finished. The Iroquois knew very little about fertilizers. As the rich soil became worn out, more land was cleared. All the land

around a village became used up after eight or ten years of growing corn. Then the people packed their belongings and moved to another place, and the clearing of the land and building of longhouses started all over again. But in spite of their poor farming methods, the Iroquois farmers raised good crops and sometimes had enough food stored away to last them several years.

The life of an Iroquois man or woman was not an easy one, even when crops were good. The women worked hard in the fields—planting, cultivating, weeding, harvesting. They cooked food, tanned deerskins, sewed clothing, wove baskets and mats, carried burdens, and raised their children. Perhaps the men had an easier time of it, for many of the daily chores were done by women. No man ever planted seed, ground corn, or carried water. But the men cleared the land and felled trees to build houses. They made the tools, carved bowls and war clubs. They hunted, fished, and went on war parties to attack the Algonkins or to defend their own homes.

In all the work the children helped, too. Older girls watched the babies and helped in the fields and in the longhouse. The babies were easy to care for. They were tied onto a cradle board, which was hung in the shade from a convenient branch. The girls learned to cook and sew, to grind corn, and to make clay pots. They shared in most of the women's work. Little girls followed their mothers about in the cornfields, holding the seed baskets, carrying away brush and weeds. They often played planting games by themselves in a corner of the field. Only the very youngest boys followed their mothers and grandmothers to the fields. Older boys preferred the company of the men and did the things the warriors liked to do.

An Iroquois boy's life was full of fun and adventure. From the time he was able to walk he was never without friends and playmates. Right in the longhouse where he lived were a dozen or more families. Most of them had children or grandchildren. Fortunately, the house was big enough for children to run around on the earth floor without getting in the way.

The Iroquois loved children and were kind to them. Iroquois boys and girls were seldom punished. If a boy got into mischief, his mother spoke quietly to him and told him to mend his ways. If he still did not behave and his mother became angry, she might throw a dipperful of water in his face. When an older boy behaved badly, his mother or grandmother threatened to put him out of the longhouse. That was a very serious matter,

since all his friends and most of his relatives lived in that house. Few boys dared to risk such a punishment. It was not the father's job to punish children.

Iroquois boys and girls had no schools. All they knew they learned by watching older people and things around them. They learned to observe everything carefully. A boy of six had a toy bow and arrow to play with, made like the big one his father used for hunting. He learned to use a blowgun, made of a straight hollow stick, and to shoot

DART

pointed darts with it just as boys use a beanshooter today. The Iroquois boy learned to stalk birds and hunt them with his blowgun. Soon his aim became almost as good as his father's.

By the time a boy was eight or nine, he was skillful enough with his blowgun and his bow and arrows to kill birds and rabbits for his mother. The older boys liked to go hunting in the woods with their friends. They formed gangs, too. Often an eight-year-old tagged along after his brothers, watching the things they did and copying them. Fights were frequent among the gangs, but they were soon forgotten, especially when adventure lay ahead. Sometimes a gang of boys stayed in the woods for several days at a time. They killed small animals, made a fire with a fire drill, and roasted their catch. This food and the parched corn they brought with them kept them well fed. Iroquois boys liked being on their own. They all wanted to become good hunters, and each looked forward to the time when his father would give a feast to celebrate his son's first successful hunt.

Boys and girls were always welcome at family gatherings and even at tribal council meetings, but they were expected to be on their best behavior. Meetings were held often in an Iroquois village. With so many families living so close together, questions often came up that could not be settled till all sides had been heard. At these gatherings the women had their say as well as the men. Since nearly everything in the Iroquois village—houses, cornfields, and stored food—belonged to the women, their opinions were important. Sometimes a woman asked her husband to speak for her. Often a woman's brother spoke for her. Older women spoke up for themselves.

As boys and girls grew up, they learned from the things they saw and the things they did. They learned how to work and to play games. They learned to dance and sing, and to enjoy the festivals and ceremonies that were the bright spots in the changing seasons. Ceremonies and festivals were fun, but they were not taken lightly. The Iroquois believed that these ceremonies helped the crops to grow, the sick to get well, and the hunters to bring home game.

The Iroquois liked to make speeches and invent songs and chants of their own. In the evenings the villagers gathered around the fires to talk. Inside the longhouse, hunters and warriors told of their deeds and adventures. They often acted out their fight with a bear or their ambush of an unsuspecting Algonkin. Everyone listened carefully, and people were sure to say, "Hah,

hah," frequently, to show that they enjoyed the story.

As the Five Nations became stronger, village life became more and more peaceful. People had less to fear as war was pushed far back into enemy territory. Warriors enjoyed the adventure of the hunt and the warpath. Women willingly performed the labor necessary for everyday living. For men, women, and children, each season brought new tasks, new adventures, and new times for fun.

2

Spring

SPRING WAS a busy season for the Iroquois. After the long cold winter, everyone—young and old—looked forward to the time they called the "renewal of life." With the very first signs of warmth, the women began the work of making maple syrup or "sweet water."

The sap of the sugar maple begins to run late in February. During the day, warmed by the spring sun, the sap flows freely. During the cold night it stops, and starts again as the air grows warm in the morning. This is the time when the sap is sweetest, as the Iroquois knew well. Maple

syrup was very important to them, since they had
no other way of sweetening their food. The syrup
made early in the spring had to last for the
whole year. Preparations for making maple syrup
began in the winter. Each family had to be sure
it owned enough bark troughs, elm-bark buckets,
and clay pots. Thirty or more quarts of sap must
be boiled to make one quart of syrup. So the villagers needed many large troughs in which to
collect the sap. They needed many pots for boiling
the sap till most of the water had boiled away
and only the thick sweet syrup remained. The
buckets were made of elm bark, folded into a
squarish box. The overlapping seams were sewed
with thread made from fibers of the basswood
tree, and were then coated with pine pitch to make
them waterproof. Women decorated these buckets
with designs of flowers, leaves, and birds. They
braided basswood cords to make handles for the
buckets and they cut strips of skin to hang the
clay cooking pots over the fires.

The large wooden troughs to hold the sap and

the cooling syrup were made by the men. They split in half a maple log five or six feet long and set the halves, flat side up, near the fire. Hot coals were set along the center of the logs to char the wood. A border of wet clay kept the edges from burning. After the center had burned, the men scraped away the charred wood and then burned the log again. Slowly, after days of work, the troughs began to take shape. Other troughs were made from large strips of elm bark, curved and folded at the ends till they were boat-shaped.

The snow at maple syrup time was still deep. The people wore fur robes and snowshoes. Every Iroquois child learned to use snowshoes and everyone could walk easily on them. There is a special knack to this, and the children learned to turn in their toes and raise each foot higher than usual at every step, gliding a bit as the snowshoe touched the ground. With snowshoes a hunter can walk as well and as fast over deep snow as he can on foot when the ground is clear.

The Maple Festival was held by the Iroquois

on the day when the tapping of the maple trees was begun. The day was chosen by the Council, so all the villages started their maple syrup work at the same time. On the first day the chief of a village and all the people went to the woods together. The Iroquois believed that the "sweet water" flowed from the maples because the trees wanted to help them. The Maple Festival was held in thanksgiving for this kindness.

When the people were assembled, the chief built a small fire under a large maple. He sprinkled some tobacco into the embers and said this simple prayer: "Partake of this tobacco, O Forest! We beg you to continue making sweet water. And may no accidents befall our children who roam the woods. This day is yours. May you enjoy it." Then the women formed a circle and the men made a larger circle around them. One man began to beat a water drum. This was made of a small hollowed log, partly filled with water, and covered with a tight buckskin. The dancers began to move round and round, in

a simple toe-heel step, keeping time to the high tone of the water drum. As they danced, they sang a chant and shook their rattles.

Meanwhile some of the men had begun to make cuts through the bark on the south side of the maple trees. They stuck a small piece of wood into each cut to act as a spout and placed a trough under each cut to catch the sap as it dripped. Later, the women went from tree to tree emptying the full troughs into bark buckets. Then they carried the watery sap to the fires which the men had built, and poured it into large clay pots. These were hung over the fires and the boiling began. It continued all through the day and often far into the night.

On the first day, while the buckets were filling, the work was light. This was a festival day which called for fun and games. The men and boys were well prepared for this. During the winter they had repaired and restrung their lacrosse sticks. A lacrosse stick is something like a hockey stick, except that there is a net on the end of it.

The player catches the ball in the net and throws it with great force from it. Lacrosse was and still is a favorite game of the Iroquois. We have learned to play lacrosse from the Indians.

On this first day of the Maple Festival the snow was tramped down over a large open field and a game of lacrosse began. The teams were not limited to twelve players as they are today. All the men and boys in the village—and they sometimes numbered as many as three and four hundred—took part in the game. When two villages played, five hundred or more men spread over the field. Women and girls often played too.

The game was rough and fast. The players raced, dodged, scooped up the deerskin ball with their netted sticks, and threw it with the practiced aim of a hunter. Players were often hurt and sometimes killed. An injured player quietly hobbled off the field and went home, very much ashamed of himself. He received little sympathy from his teammates. The Iroquois thought it a disgrace to get hurt while playing a game.

To the Iroquois lacrosse was more than just a sport. A person who was ill might be cured by watching a lacrosse game. A good game might please the spirits who favored it so much that they would drive away famine and disease. There

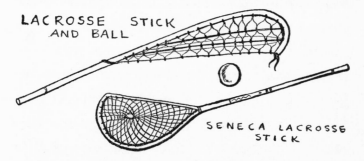

LACROSSE STICK
AND BALL

SENECA LACROSSE
STICK

was no greater honor for a visitor or a chief than to have a game of lacrosse played because of his visit.

At the edge of the woods fires were kept burning while the game went on. The pots of maple sap bubbled and boiled. Toward evening the syrup began to thicken. Then it was poured into the cooling troughs. The women ladled some of the thickened syrup out onto the snow, where it quickly hardened into maple sugar candy. This was given to the impatient children, who kept returning to the fires from the game, eager for the treat.

By now it was getting dark. Everyone was happy, but tired and hungry. All the people moved over to the fires. The women ladled out bowls of hot syrup. They passed around corn-meal cakes they had baked and brought along. Everyone enjoyed the cakes and syrup, while they talked about the first lacrosse game of the season. They argued and joked until late at night. As each person finished the last drop of syrup in his bowl, he said aloud, as in prayer, "I am thankful."

Now the fires were dying and the troughs of maple syrup were nearly empty. However, the first day's run of sap had been good and the women knew it would flow again tomorrow and for another two or three weeks. There would be enough sweet water to drink and plenty to store away in clay pots for flavoring their food.

As long as the sap flowed, the women and girls went to the woods each day. Fires were kept going and the troughs of sap were emptied into the clay pots as fast as they filled. Potfuls of maple syrup were taken to the village each night, covered with pieces of buckskin, and stored away.

Toward the end of maple-syrup time, the snow was almost gone and the women no longer wore snowshoes. The paths in the woods and in the village were wet and muddy. The women stuffed dry moss in their moccasins and changed them during the day, to keep their feet dry.

When the ground had thawed in the spring sun and "the leaf on the dogwood grew to the size of a squirrel's ear," the time for planting had arrived. Before dawn on the first day of planting, young girls went to the fields with little baskets of corn. Each girl threw a few grains over her family's fields, as a gesture of thanks to the Great Spirit and a prayer for a good harvest. Later in the day, the women and children trooped to the fields with their digging sticks, hoes, and seed baskets.

Corn was more precious than good soil to the

early Iroquois farmers. Good corn seed was hard to get. A warrior did not hesitate to travel a hundred miles to trade for good corn seed to bring back to the village. After each harvest the women carefully put away ears of corn to be used for next year's planting. This seed corn was never eaten, no matter how short of food a family might be at the end of the year. The Iroquois had at least five kinds of corn—white, black, yellow, red, and popcorn. Each family planted some of each kind, but more white corn than any of the others.

Planting was women's work. An Iroquois man would rather go hungry than be seen in the fields. The women dug the soil, planted, weeded, and harvested the crops. Women and girls worked in groups with their digging sticks and hoes. One woman loosened the soil; another dug holes one big step apart; a third dropped three kernels of corn into each hole. These were covered with a mixture of soil and crushed shells, which gave the plants some extra lime.

In between the mounds of corn the women

planted squashes, pumpkins, and gourds. They also planted rows of native tobacco, sunflowers, and beans.

Sunflower seeds were an important food for the Iroquois and were probably used before they learned to grow corn. They first gathered wild sunflowers. Later they grew them from seed. When the sunflowers were ripe, the seeds were taken out and pounded into a pulp. The oil was drained off and used in cooking and for flavoring bread. It was also fed to babies. Sunflowers, like corn, were unknown in Europe before the discovery of America. Today sunflowers are more important in some parts of Europe than they are here, where their seeds were first used as a food.

Tobacco was another important crop. It, too, was a wild plant long before it was cultivated. Whenever people gathered around a fire, a few crushed dry tobacco leaves were thrown into the embers, because everyone liked the smell of the tobacco smoke. Later, the Iroquois learned to make stone and clay pipes and to smoke tobacco. However, the old customs were not forgotten. At a festival or council fire, a chief usually sprinkled tobacco over the coals as an offering to the spirits. The Iroquois believed that the spirits liked the smell of tobacco. They also believed that no matter how far away the spirits might be, they would come as soon as they smelled the tobacco smoke.

The work of growing food and preparing meals was done by the women. Corn was the chief crop raised and was also the main food, eaten at every meal. A large part of Iroquois food was made up of soups and puddings—corn soup, corn-meal mush, corn pudding, hominy, and so on. Corn meal cooked with beans made succotash, a favorite Iroquois dish. Fresh and dried berries and nuts, meat and fat, and smoked fish were added to the soups and puddings. Maple syrup was often added for sweetening. Iroquois women could cook about forty different corn dishes.

The Iroquois did not have salt. Yet, oddly enough, one of the largest salt deposits in the world lies deep underground below the Iroquois territory. Later, when traders brought them salt, the Iroquois took a liking to it, and the women wove little salt containers out of cornhusks to hold this valuable seasoning.

To prepare corn for food, the dry kernels were ground into corn meal. In the mornings the whole village was filled with the sound of the heavy wooden pestles pounding up and down in the large mortars. The mortars were logs about three feet high, hollowed at one end. The women dropped

shelled corn into the mortars and pounded it until it broke down into meal. The meal was sifted through a loosely woven sieve and was added to boiling water to make corn-meal mush.

Parched corn meal was used a great deal by the Iroquois. After corn was shelled, it was put on a hot stone and roasted. Then it was ground into meal to make parched corn meal. Hunters and warriors always carried pouches of parched corn meal.

It took longer to make corn bread than corn pudding, because corn bread was made of flour, not meal. To make flour, an Iroquois woman put a pot of freshly shelled corn on the fire to boil. In another pot, she added boiling water to wood ashes to soak out the potash and lye. After the hulls had loosened from the boiled corn, she heated it again in the lye solution until each kernel had bleached and swelled. Then, with a woven scoop, she lifted the kernels out of the lye and dumped them into a large trough of cold water. When the lye had washed out, the white, plump kernels were spread on mats to dry. Then they were ready to be stored, cooked as hominy, or ground into flour.

To make boiled corn bread, the flour was mixed with water in a wooden trough, kneaded into dough, and patted into flat cakes. These were slipped carefully into a large pot of boiling water and served hot on a tray. Sometimes the flat cakes were baked in hot ashes.

The Iroquois enjoyed strawberries, blackberries, and other fruits and berries. They ate wild plants in addition to those they grew, and also nuts. When hunters brought down a deer, elk, moose, or sometimes a buffalo, everyone had plenty of meat. The fresh meat was cut up and boiled in puddings. It was also broiled over the fire on a pointed stick. Dried and smoked meat or fish was first boiled to soften it a bit and then pounded in a mortar to a hash, to be cooked with the corn meal. Meat pounded with fat and berries was taken along by hunters and warriors together with their pouches of parched corn.

Except at a festival, the Iroquois ate only one
meal a day—in the morning. The family sat or
stood around the fire, each with his own spoon
and bowl. The men and boys were served first
from the clay pot in the embers. Then the women

and girls had their turn. Leftover food was kept
in the pot by the fire so that anyone who felt
hungry during the day could help himself. A
visitor was always welcome to share whatever
was in the pot. Dishes were not washed. They
were scraped with a few cornhusks and allowed
to dry. After a while the bowls and spoons became so coated with grease that they turned a
deep, shiny brown.

Many of the family activities centered in the Iroquois longhouse. This huge building was aptly named, for it might be from fifty to one hundred and fifty feet long and some twenty to twenty-five feet wide. A half dozen to ten families—sometimes as many as fifty people—lived in this bark-covered, single-story barn with a sloping roof and a door at each end. Longhouses had neither windows nor chimneys. Openings in the roof let out some of the smoke from the cooking fires, but the inside of the longhouse was always dark, smoky, and full of the strong odors of cooking, of drying meat, of skins, and of people.

The men built the frame of the longhouse with logs and poles, lashed together with bark ropes. Sheets of elm and hickory bark were peeled off in early spring and flattened with heavy stones. After these sheets dried, they were tied over the frame of the longhouse. The bark was held in place by smaller poles. The two entrances were covered with skins. At best, a newly finished longhouse looked uneven and shaggy, but it was

roomy and often comfortable. In winter the women filled the chinks in the walls with dried moss and grass to keep out the wind.

Down the center of the earth floor of the longhouse was a row of small fire pits. Two families usually shared the same fire. In warm weather some of the women prepared their meals outdoors. But in winter the families ate by the fire and pulled over their sleeping mats and furs to sleep as close to the embers as possible.

Poles were lashed across the rafters near the roof on both sides of the longhouse. These were used for storage. Other stronger platforms, about twelve feet long and six feet wide, were built along the walls a foot or two from the floor. These platforms were the Iroquois beds. The space under them was also used for storage.

With so many families in one house, each had only a small space to call its own. This was screened with skins, so a tired hunter or a sick person could rest quietly, if one can imagine quiet with women working, children running and playing, and half-tamed dogs barking. Yet despite this crowding, the people in the longhouse got along very well with each other and did not get in each other's way.

Some of the food belonging to each family was stored in its living quarters. Strings of corn and dried meat hung from the rafters. Bunches of clean-smelling sweet grass hung from the poles. Pots and baskets of corn, dried berries, and other stored food overflowed the space under the sleeping platform. Each family had several clay cooking pots, bowls, sieves, spoons, ladles, troughs, and

other utensils. Each had stone tools for cutting, chopping, grinding, and scraping, and a large supply of cornhusks and mats. Besides all this, the men hung their bows and war clubs, their snow-shoes, belts, charms, and pouches along the walls. Every bit of the crowded space was used.

The Iroquois had no chairs or tables. They sat on the sleeping platforms. On the sleeping platform each member of a family had his own sleeping place. The bedding usually consisted of a thick, soft cornhusk mat covered with skins and

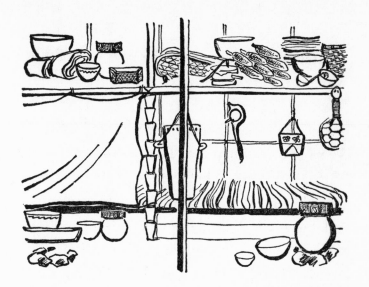

furs. A baby slept next to its mother or in a tiny hammock made of cornhusks that hung over the mother's sleeping place. In the morning, the mother or older sister picked up the baby and put fresh dry moss, which served as an Iroquois diaper, in its buckskin blanket. The baby was wrapped tightly in buckskin and tied to the cradle board with crossed buckskin straps. The baby's feet rested on a foot board. The cradle board was hung on a pole outside the sleeping compartment while the mother was busy cooking.

After the morning meal the boys went fishing or joined a gang heading for the woods with their blowguns and bows and arrows. Some of the men took up their mesh baskets, dip nets, and harpoons and went off fishing, too. The Iroquois were very skillful fishermen. They used traps and nets with stone sinkers. It was a favorite sport of theirs to go out at night, light a fire on the shore of a lake, and spear eels as they came up to the light. This sport is still popular with the Iroquois today.

Other men stayed in the village. Some took their stone hatchets and went off to get wood for bows and gather stalks of arrowwood and osier for arrow shafts. Older men sat in the sun, flaking chert and flint to make drill points and arrowheads. The women and girls took up their seed baskets and cradle boards and started back to the cornfields to plant, weed, or cultivate the corn.

3

Summer

As spring gave way to the hot summer months, the women spent more time in the village than they did during the busy planting season. Already the corn was knee high and the growing crops needed less care. A few women went out to the fields to weed and cultivate. If the fields were dry, the women carried water to the young squash and pumpkins.

Overhead in the longhouses the rafters showed more and more empty spaces, as the last of the stored corn, beans, and dried meat was used up. Already some Cayuga warriors had borrowed corn and beans from their neighbors in the Onondaga and Seneca villages. Now the villagers were looking ahead to the harvest of wild and cultivated crops that would soon be ready. New baskets and new clay pots must be made.

The Iroquois made excellent clay pots for cooking and storage. They were shaped by hand and this took a great deal of skill. A good potter soon became known from one end of the Iroquois territory to the other. Only pure fine clay was used. The clay was moistened till it was just right for molding. A long coil of clay was then rolled out. This coil was twisted round and round, patted and smoothed with wet hands. The coiling began with the rounded bottom. Next the curved sides were built up and smoothed with a pebble or polished bone. The rim of the pot was flattened and a design was scratched into the wide border with a fingernail or a piece of bone. The pots were set out in the sun to dry. They were then covered with hot embers till the clay was baked hard.

The pots the Iroquois women made all had a

wide decorated rim and round bottom. They were of various sizes. Storage pots usually held several gallons. Cooking pots held a gallon or two. Pots broke easily and the women were kept busy making new ones. When the traders came with their copper pots and iron kettles, the Iroquois were overjoyed to get them. They soon stopped making clay pots and the art of pottery was almost forgotten.

The men gathered the raw material for making baskets. They chose a young black or white ash with the lower trunk free of branches. Some cut down the tree and peeled the bark from the trunk. Others pounded the wood with stone hammers or wooden mallets till it split around the growth rings. With a sharp piece of bone or flint, the men cut through each layer of wood and peeled it off. They cut the thin wood into long strips. While the strips were still fresh and pliable, the women wove them into baskets. The girls helped, working side by side with their mothers and grandmothers. At first a girl made small simple baskets.

But as she became more skilled, she made larger ones with more attractive designs.

The women made strong cord out of twisted basswood fiber. Basswood fibers were also used to braid the special strap that was attached to burden baskets. The women carried these baskets on their backs and put the strap or tumpline, as it was called, across the forehead and back over their shoulders when carrying a load. Often a plain tumpline was not good enough. Some women embroidered theirs with moose hair and porcupine quills. The designs were always attractive, for an Iroquois woman believed that a pretty tumpline and a well-made basket made her burden easier to carry.

Women also made dyes to color their baskets and tumplines. They dyed moose hair and porcupine quills and used these to ornament moccasins, belts, and clothing. Some of the Iroquois dyes were made from red and yellow iron ore found in the rocks. Most of them, however, were made from plants. The women knew these plants and

went out to gather bloodroot, sumac, butternut, and yellowroot. The plants were boiled till the color came out into the water. Then the basket strips, the porcupine quills, or the twisted cords were dyed. The colors were neither strong nor brilliant, but they lasted well.

Before the European traders came, the Iroquois had no metal. Women made clothing using sharpened pieces of bone for needles. An Iroquois woman punched hole after hole in folded buckskin to make a seam. Then she carefully pulled thread made of sinews through the holes. She also punched holes along the seams and borders, and pulled moose hair or porcupine quills through till she worked out a colorful design. Sometimes, as another kind of ornament, bunches of human hair were sewed on the front and back of a shirt. When an Iroquois boy killed a porcupine in the woods and brought it home to his mother, she pulled out the quills and sorted them for size. The smaller quills were dyed with vegetable dyes. The boy's reward might be a pair of new moccasins or perhaps a wide buckskin belt and pouch, decorated with the porcupine quills.

Iroquois moccasins were almost perfect footwear for people who lived as the Iroquois did. Long after they began to use metal and cloth, and

TUMPLINE
and
BURDEN
BASKET

even after they had given up living in their longhouses, they still wore these soft buckskin moccasins. An Iroquois moccasin was made of a single piece of buckskin with the seam running from the toe up to the instep. The moccasins were decorated with porcupine-quill designs. Because the moccasins were soft-soled, they soon wore through. Women patched and patched till the soles were past patching. Then a new pair was brought out.

A good housewife had several pairs of moccasins on hand for every member of her family. She often took the decorated tops off a pair of worn moccasins and put them on a new pair.

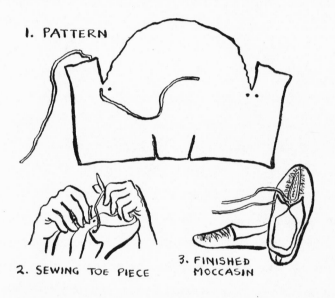

1. PATTERN

2. SEWING TOE PIECE

3. FINISHED MOCCASIN

When work in the fields or around the long-house slowed down, there was always sewing for Iroquois women to do. Rolls of buckskins lay on the storage platforms, ready to be made into clothing and moccasins. The longhouse was dark and cold in winter, so summer afternoons were the best time for sewing.

The clothing that the Iroquois women made was very practical. In summer very little clothing was worn. Men wore a breechcloth and moccasins. A breechcloth was made of a long strip of buckskin, tucked between the legs and looped over a belt. The ends of the breechcloth reached to the knees in front and back. The women wore a short buckskin skirt. Young children wore nothing at all. The older ones dressed like their parents.

In colder weather, of course, more clothing was needed. Both men and women wore buckskin leggings which covered their legs and thighs. These were tied by thongs to the belt and below the knees. Buckskin shirts were added, too. The woman's shirt was usually longer and more decorated than the man's knee-length shirt. Fur hats were used in winter, as well as extra fur sleeves and capes or blankets made of furs or skins.

For feasts and festivals everyone wore his best clothing, heavy with embroidery and decorations.

Necklaces of perforated shells, animal teeth, and bone beads were proudly displayed. Hair was slicked down with bear grease. Those who wore

DEERSKIN LEGGINGS

their hair long had two long braids which hung down in front. Warriors, as a challenge to the enemy, often cut their hair very close, leaving only a long tuft or scalp lock on the crown. This lock was ornamented on festive days with a few turkey feathers or with the dyed tail of a deer.

Everyone was proud of handsome clothes for

festivals. Fine buckskins were proof that a woman was an industrious worker and her husband a good hunter. A mother and grandmother worked for weeks to decorate a shirt for a boy or girl. This was

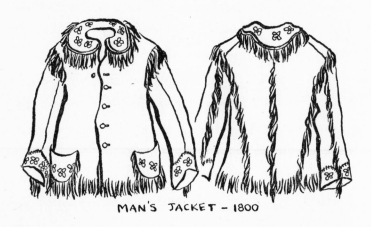

MAN'S JACKET - 1800

one of the ways in which adults showed their love for their children. Family ties were very strong with the Iroquois and still are today.

The families in a longhouse were always willing to help one another, both because that was the custom and because they were usually related. Relatives were expected to work together and to share food and other possessions. Sisters, even after they had married, continued to live in the same longhouse, raising their families and working together. A boy called his mother's sister "Mother" instead of "Aunt." Cousins called each other "Brother" or "Sister." But a boy called his father's sister "Aunt" and her husband "Uncle." A girl who did not have a baby brother or sister helped care for a baby cousin whom she called "Little Brother." She loved him as much as she would her own brother. A boy of ten or twelve took a younger boy along when he headed for the woods with his gang. "This is my younger brother, Little Bear," he told the others, even though Little Bear was not his real brother but the son of his mother's sister. This way of living together made the families seem much larger.

The older women in the family—the mother and grandmother—gave orders, and the younger ones listened respectfully and obeyed. The fathers seldom interfered with the younger children. When they were hungry cr wanted permission to go to the woods, they spoke to their mother. Girls stayed closer to the mother than boys, but both depended on her for care and help. However, when a boy entered his teens and was ready to go hunting with the men, his father took charge of him and taught him the ways of the hunt and the warpath. Every boy trained for about a year to become fit for a life of hunting and warfare. During this time he lived alone in a small hut outside the village. His grandfather or grandmother cared for him and saw to it that he trained hard. In both summer and winter, after his daily run a boy had to plunge into a nearby stream. He ate sparingly and sometimes fasted. When this training period ended, an Iroquois boy was hardened for any emergency.

The Iroquois tribes were divided into clans, usually named after an animal or bird. The clans of each tribe were Bear, Wolf, Turtle, Beaver, Deer, Snipe, Heron, Hawk, and Eel. People of the same clan considered themselves blood relatives, whether they actually were or not. Two people of the same clan could not marry. If a man of the

Bear clan married a woman of the Snipe clan, their children belonged to the Snipe clan. So a child felt closer to the mother's relatives than to the father's. The father's relatives lived in another longhouse and sometimes in a different village. They belonged to a different clan, the Bears. Members of a clan in one Iroquois tribe were sure of a welcome from members of the same clan in any of the villages of other Iroquois tribes.

When an Iroquois woman had a child, she asked an old woman of her clan to help her find a "free" name for the baby. A "free" name was a name that was not in use at the moment. It might have belonged to a relative who gave it up to take on a more important name, or the name might have belonged to a person who had recently died. A mother always chose her children's names, but she asked the help of an older, wiser woman because she wanted a good name, one that would help the child. An Iroquois mother wanted her son to grow up to be a good hunter and a leader

of his tribe. She wanted her daughter to be industrious but quiet and shy, as an Iroquois girl
should be. So the mother sought a name that
would help her child and set it a good example.
A boy who was given the name of a famous hunter,
warrior, or chief of the clan tried to follow in his
footsteps. A girl who had the name of a famous
potter or of a woman who made beautiful baskets
was very proud of it. She tried to follow in her
namesake's footsteps. As she grew older, the girl
took on the famous woman's other name. For each
Iroquois had several names.

A woman of the Turtle clan, for example, had
a baby boy and went for advice to the old woman
who was Keeper of the Names. A famous warrior
of the Turtle clan, named Destroy-village, had
died the year before. When Destroy-village was
a baby he had been called Swimmer. So the two
women decided to call the baby boy Swimmer.
After Swimmer grew up, he changed his name
to Destroy-village. When Destroy-village was
ready to marry, his mother and grandmother

selected a bride for him from another clan, the Wolves. Then Destroy-village of the Turtle clan went to live with his wife in the longhouse of the Wolf clan, and his children belonged to the Wolf clan. But Destroy-village remained a member of the Turtle clan. He never forgot his relatives and his relatives did not forget him. He always stopped off to see them when he went hunting and passed their village. If his children needed help, they could get it not only from their relatives in the Wolf clan but also from their father's relatives, the Turtles.

This way of thinking about relatives was quite different from ours. So was the Iroquois custom of adopting people into the family and the tribe. If a family lost a son or a daughter, they tried to find an orphan to adopt. A feast was held and the boy or girl was given a suitable clan name. From then on the child was called by this name and was considered a member of the clan and tribe, just as though he or she had been born a member.

When warriors returned from the warpath,

they often brought captives back with them. Families adopted some of these captives to replace men who had been killed. Even though the captive had recently been an enemy, when he was adopted into the tribe he became an Iroquois. From then on he was expected to act like an Iroquois warrior in everything he did.

At first Iroquois tribes warred against one another, every tribe for itself. Then, after the League of the Five Nations was formed, the Iroquois concentrated on the Algonkins, till some were wiped out and others retreated farther north into Canada. Around 1650 the Iroquois were at the height of their power.

Wars, as the Iroquois fought them before they had guns, were really surprise raids by a war party on a village or camp of another tribe. They did not consider raiding as stealing. It was a good thing to fight a tribe that did not belong to the League of Five Nations. An adventurous Iroquois warrior might ask some of his close relatives and friends to join him in a raid on an Algonkin camp he had observed while on a hunt. Several young men would at once agree to go along. If the leader thought his party was large enough, they started at once. If not, the raid was talked over with the warriors of another longhouse. The leader told of his plans and asked for warriors to fill out the party. A man often went along, even though he had good reasons for staying behind, because he feared he would be considered a coward by the others if he refused.

An Iroquois war party departed in secret. They traveled light and fast. Each warrior carried little else besides his pouch of parched corn, his war club tucked into his embroidered belt, and his bow and arrows. Sometimes Iroquois warriors carried armor made of wooden slats tied with fibers, to protect the chest and back. Their hickory bow was short, about four and a half feet long, but heavy. It took a strong, practiced arm to pull it. Arrows were made of red osier or arrowwood. They were tipped with heads of flaked chert or quartz bound to the shaft with sinew. Each arrow was

feathered with goose, duck, hawk, or turkey feathers, and was tested carefully to make sure it was straight and true. The war party followed the well-known paths that the tribes had used as long as they could remember. They walked in single file behind the leader, as they did in hunting, but they moved faster and kept a careful lookout to see that they were not observed. A war party traveled by canoe if they lived near the larger rivers or lakes.

Iroquois made and used elm-bark canoes. They

were much cruder than the famed birchbark canoes made by other Eastern Indians. There were few birch trees in the lands of the Iroquois, but elms were abundant. To make a canoe, a length of bark was removed from the thick trunk of an elm. Ribs were inserted into the piece of bark. At both bow and stern the edges of the bark were sewed together. The seams and any cracks in the bark were sealed with pitch to make the canoe watertight. The elm-bark canoe was not as fast nor as silent as the birchbark canoe, but it worked

well enough. The Iroquois warriors were skilled
in using these rather clumsy canoes.

Once near the enemy camp, the war party hid
their canoes or left the trails, and worked their

ELM BARK CANOE

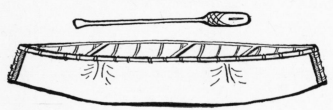

way closer under the protection of the forest.
Without warning, they attacked in the middle
of the night or just before dawn when the enemy
was still asleep. Rushing in wildly under cover of
darkness, the whooping Iroquois wakened the
sleeping camp. Women and children ran for the
woods. Men seized their weapons and fought the
attackers. Some were made prisoners. Many fell
under the blows of the Iroquois war clubs. Warriors on both sides scalped those they had killed.
Scalps were proof of their courage, so the war-

rior who took the most was known as the bravest.

The war party departed as quickly as it had
come, hustling prisoners ahead of them. The prisoners were loaded with the skins and other prizes
the victors had taken. The party could not slow
down or rest on its return trip for fear of being
overtaken by pursuing Algonkins before they
reached their own territory. When the warriors
finally got back to their village, they were greeted
with joyous shouts. The women promptly tied
the scalps to poles and paraded around the village, singing the praises of the men who had risked
their lives on the warpath.

Before the Five Nations became stronger than
any of their neighbors, every village knew that
sooner or later the Algonkins would return to
avenge their losses. This is why the Iroquois villages were built with walls around them. Before
the harvest, warriors watched over the cornfields
day and night. If a raiding party of Algonkins
set fire to the cornfields at harvest time, the winter would be a hard one in the village.

Next to hunting and the warpath, the Iroquois warriors enjoyed trading. Trading meant barter, since the Iroquois had no coins or money. An Iroquois warrior traded his possessions—necklaces, arrows, embroidered leather belt and pouches—for the things he wanted. It was much easier to organize a trading party than either a war party or a hunt. The women were interested in trading too, but since they were too busy to leave the village they asked the men to trade for them, and told them exactly what they expected to get. Later, when European traders visited the villages, the women did most of the trading.

Trading went on continuously among the Five Nations. Buckskins and baskets changed hands. One kind of corn was exchanged for another. Embroidered moccasins were traded for war clubs or a special bow. Dried meat was traded for squash. This trading was usually peaceful. The arguments were part of the fun. If any serious argument arose, the tribal chiefs or even the Council of the League stepped in to settle differences.

The adventurous Iroquois went farther and farther afield on their trading expeditions. These trips took them out of their own territory as far east as the Atlantic coast. Here they traded with the Indians of Long Island for wampum. Wampum are tiny beads made from clam shells. Dark purple wampum was valued much higher than white, but the Iroquois valued both. Strings of wampum became prized possessions and were the nearest thing to money the Iroquois had. Wampum strings acquired many uses because they were so valued. Official messengers, calling the chiefs to assemble in council or carrying tidings from the League, carried strings of wampum as signs of their authority. Treaties were made official and were recorded by wampum belts, made especially for the occasion.

The Iroquois also traded with the Algonkins with whom they fought. Toward the end of summer or in the fall the tribes would declare a truce. Messengers arranged the time, and warriors of both tribes met to exchange furs and dried meat for tobacco, corn, beans, and canoes. Sometimes the truce was broken and the trading ended in a pitched battle, while the goods were scattered and destroyed as the warriors fought.

For nearly two hundred years after the first explorers reached the Iroquois, trading with the Europeans became more and more important. The Iroquois household began to depend on trade goods: metal needles, thimbles, iron kettles, wax candles. The warriors wanted tomahawks and knives as well as firearms. The Dutch, French, and English all wanted furs, and the Iroquois and other tribes were urged to trap and shoot all the animals they could. Traders, who came to trade with the Indians, often cheated them. But the Iroquois seldom argued. After a dishonest trader left, a few of the men, freshly painted for the warpath, caught up with him. They took back all their furs as well as all his trade goods. The trader was lucky to get back to the fort with his scalp.

When furs became important, much of the trading was done in the spring after the winter hunting and trapping was over. Before that time, more of the trading was done in late summer and fall, after crops had ripened and the men had more time and more goods on hand. For the Iroquois, as for all other people who live on the soil, the fall was a time of harvest, a time of prosperity and plenty.

4

Fall

THE IROQUOIS did not have a calendar as we do, and they did not reckon time accurately till they learned how to do it from the Europeans. Instead they named each season for the important activities that went on at that particular time: planting in spring, for example; harvesting and hunting in fall. Each important activity began with a festival, so the different seasons of the year were easy for all the people to remember.

Beginning in summer and going on into the fall, the gathering of berries was an important task. Thanksgiving festivals were held as each kind of berry ripened and was gathered by the women. Berries were a tasty food that every Iroquois liked. Strawberries, blackberries, raspberries, elderberries, and blueberries were gathered. The Iroquois believed that cranberries and huckleberries were good for the blood and for the liver, so these were always a special treat.

Berries were plentiful along the edges of the woods and in open fields. Abandoned cornfields became excellent berry patches. As each kind of berry ripened, the women went out to gather them. Each took along three baskets. Two small baskets bound together with a buckskin thong were thrown over one shoulder. A woman also carried a large basket in one hand. Berry picking was not as hard as the women's other work and it was a kind of holiday for them.

Each woman worked fast and skillfully. First

she filled the basket that hung over her shoulder in front. When this was filled, she reversed the baskets and continued till both were filled. Then she emptied the two small baskets into her large basket. If everything went well, a woman might go back to the village at nightfall with all her baskets filled to the brim with berries. When a young girl succeeded in filling all her baskets she was very happy. The older women praised her and told everyone in the village what a good worker she was.

A good many of the berries were eaten fresh. Some were crushed and mixed with corn mush or corn pudding. Part of each crop was spread in the sun to dry and then was stored for winter use. Dried berries were pounded with meat and fat to make a nourishing food for hunters and warriors to carry with them. Dried berries soaked in water and sweetened with maple syrup made a fine drink. Dried berries soaked in water were also used in soups, puddings, and breads.

Berry picking began in June when the strawberries ripened. The Iroquois called strawberries "the first fruit of the earth," and the Strawberry Festival was eagerly awaited. Like the Maple Festival, it began with a prayer of thanks as a chief sprinkled tobacco over a fire. Again the villagers sang, danced, and played games.

The game of darts was often added to the usual game of lacrosse. Two teams of fifteen to thirty players each were chosen. Each player had a half-dozen wooden spears about five feet long, made of slender sticks of hickory or maple. The players stood in line and the umpires, a short distance away, rolled an eight-inch reed hoop in front of them. Each player in turn tried to throw his spear through the hoop as it rolled by. If he succeeded, the umpires took his spear away. When every man on one team had thrown his spear, the other team had its turn. The team that lost all its spears first was the winner.

Sometimes the spears were thrown for distance and the one who threw the farthest was the winner. But the scoring was still by teams and the team with the most winners was the victor. Excitement always ran high, for everyone who could afford it made bets on the different teams. The men placed their bets with the umpires. They put up their most valued possessions: strings of wampum, embroidered belts, pouches, pipes, and tobacco. The umpires watched over the bets and saw that they were fairly distributed among those who won.

A strawberry feast was held after the games. Everyone ate crushed berries mixed with maple syrup and topped off with corn pudding—a kind of strawberry shortcake.

Later in the summer, when the sweet corn was ripe enough to eat, a Green Corn Festival was held with similar ceremonies. Then everyone ate fresh

corn pudding to their heart's content. The Green Corn Festival was the biggest of the summer season. The games and feasting lasted for four days.

Fall was the nut-gathering season. Again the women spent many days in the woods, gathering the nuts as they ripened. Hickory and chestnut were the favorites. They also gathered acorns, black walnuts, butternuts, and hazelnuts.

The women used boulders with small hollows in them for cracking the nuts. A nut was set in the hollow and hit with a stone. The fresh nut meats were put in wooden bowls and ground fine. The ground nut meal was then boiled in water. The oil from the nuts came to the surface and was skimmed off with a ladle, just as we skim the cream off milk. This oil was stored in clay pots. Hickory-nut oil was used in flavoring succotash and in making bread. This and butternut oil were fed to babies.

The boiled nut meal was not wasted. It was mixed in puddings. So were the mealy chestnuts, which contained very little oil. Hulled dried chestnuts were pounded into flour and mixed with corn flour to give the bread more flavor.

In the early fall months the older women gathered roots that would be used for medicine and for dyes. All sorts of wild plants good for injuries and ailments were sought for in the woods. Twigs of the Juneberry bush were collected and dried.

These were boiled to make a tea to cure an upset stomach. So were the twigs of sassafras and witch hazel. The old women knew which plants were safe to eat and which were poisonous, and they taught the younger people which to collect and which to avoid. The good mushrooms and puff-balls were picked and cooked. Wild onions and garlic were gathered and mixed with nut oil and sunflower oil. These mixtures were used in flavoring meat. Even after the Iroquois learned to use salt they gathered these plants to flavor their bread, corn, and meat.

And now the real rush began. Fall was half-way over. Ripening fields of corn, sunflowers, beans, pumpkin, squash, and gourds promised an abundant harvest. There would be long hours of work before all the harvest could be gathered. The women, baskets on their backs, hurried to the fields early every morning. They broke the ears of corn from the stalks and threw them into large harvesting baskets. Hundreds of bushels of corn were picked and carted back up the long hill to the village. Sometimes, when the harvest was heavier than usual, the cornstalks were uprooted and dragged to the village. There they were piled in crossed layers to await husking at a later, less busy time.

MAN
PLAYING A
WATER DRUM

When that time came, the picked corn was not all husked. Instead, on some of the ears the husks were peeled back and braided together till a dozen or twenty ears of corn hung in a long heavy string. The men helped with this. Some pitched in just to show the women how fast they could work. The older men sat in groups around the fires, carving or smoking. One played a small water drum, while another shook two rattles and sang.

Moved by the drum, the rattles, and the singing, several young men and women formed two lines by the fire and danced, stamping out their steps as they moved in two small circles. Older boys who knew the steps trailed along after them, imitating every movement. Over at one side some younger boys twisted cornhusks into clubs and started a battle. Another gang with cornstalk spears attacked, yelling their war whoops. The battle became so noisy that an older woman stopped her work and told the boys to quiet down.

As it grew darker, an old warrior started telling a story of a raid he had been in. Everyone fell silent and listened. Mothers and grandmothers stopped husking corn and held the younger children. One took up a few husks of corn and quickly made a doll with them for a sleepy child. Cornhusk dolls were favorites with Iroquois children. They were made by twisting and folding husks into a head, body, arms, and legs. The little dolls were always made without faces. If the doll had a face, the Iroquois believed, it might turn into a real person. An older girl might make clothing and moccasins for a child's doll.

CORN HUSK DOLL

Cornstalks and cornhusks were not thrown away. The Iroquois had many uses for them. From crushed green cornstalks they made a lotion that was applied to cuts and bruises. A cut finger was wrapped in a clean dry cornhusk bandage. The tassel stems were cut and dried. Boys and girls played with them and learned to count. Single cornhusks were folded and twisted into a thin tight lamplighter. A burning lamp-

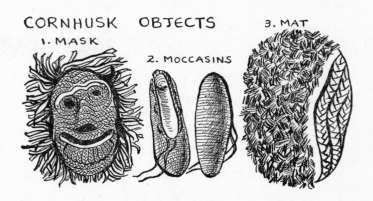

CORNHUSK OBJECTS

1. MASK

2. MOCCASINS

3. MAT

lighter could be carried a short distance from one fire to light another. Dried cornhusks were used as kindling to nurse the spark from a fire drill into a flame.

Around the longhouse cornhusks were used all the time. Girls braided them to make clothes-lines. Braided hammocks for babies were hung over the mothers' sleeping platforms. Moccasins were woven out of husks for summer wear. Mats to sleep on were made of braided husks, and so were door mats. Corncobs were used by the old men to make pipe bowls. They used corncobs for back scratchers and hand brushes. Young corncobs were ground up and eaten. The women also used them for scrubbing. Dried corncobs made the fires for smoking fish, meat, and hides, and for use in firing clay pots. Kernels of corn were strung and used by both men and women as necklaces. The pulp of green corn was used in tanning skins.

As the harvest progressed, the look of the long-house changed. Fresh strings of corn hung once again from the rafters. When the rafters were filled, the men put up poles outside and hung the corn on these to dry. New mats appeared and bundles of cornhusks were piled up for future use. Storage pots were refilled and stored again under the sleeping platforms.

The Iroquois also stored dried and parched corn in large pits that were lined and covered with bark and cornhusks. They stored their squash and pumpkins in pits, too. These fruits, thus protected from freezing, kept right through the cold winter. Tobacco leaves, picked earlier in the fall, were tied in bundles and hung to dry from the rafters of the longhouse.

The Iroquois had a double reason to be thankful for this plentiful supply of food. They had enough to eat and they would be able to trade some of their harvest for skins and furs. The Iroquois men looked forward to the trading and to the hunting ahead of them.

With the coming of colder weather, the men began to organize hunting parties. Each party was made up of two or three or sometimes a dozen men, under the leadership of a chief who was an experienced hunter. A father was proud to take his son along with him. The young man who was taken on a hunt for the first time had a chance to prove what a good hunter he was.

A hunting party often planned to stay away for several months, from early fall till the Midwinter Festival. Preparations were carefully made. The men had to carry food, weapons, and extra moccasins. Yet the hunters tried to travel light because they traveled far and fast. Sometimes a party covered thirty miles a day when scouting for game. Parties of Iroquois hunters often went far from home. They went down into what is now Ohio, a favorite hunting ground. They moved up into the Niagara Peninsula, where game was known to be plentiful, and down the Susquehanna River into Pennsylvania, as far south as the Potomac. They went to the headwaters of the

Delaware River and east to Lake Champlain.
Other parties crossed into Canada.

Sometimes when a hunting party did not expect
to cover much ground, the wives went along.
They built shelters of hemlock boughs. While
the men were out hunting, the women cooked
and took care of the game the hunters had already
killed.

A hunting party usually followed one of the
well-worn Indian trails that covered most of the
eastern part of this country. They moved in single
file behind their leader, stopping only for short
rests and for a few mouthfuls of parched corn
and water.

Once game was sighted by scouts who had
been sent ahead, the party scattered through the
woods. These hunters knew the habits of deer, elk,
moose, and bear. When hunting deer, elk, and
moose, a hunter stationed himself at a salt lick or
a place where he knew deer came down to drink.
He only shot his arrow when the animal came
within range. Hunters seldom carried more than

two dozen arrows apiece, so they could not afford to waste any. Each one hoped to make a kill and recover the arrows he had used.

There was no way to be sure that a hunt would be successful. Sometimes game was scarce; sometimes it was plentiful. When an animal was killed, it was first skinned. The skin was smoked to preserve it, and then stretched out to dry. Other hunters cut up the animal. Some of the meat was cooked and eaten on the spot. The rest was boned, cut into small strips, and hung up to smoke over the fire. The bones, entrails, and leftovers from cooking were placed carefully near a rock, so the little wood spirits who, the Iroquois believed, also hunted in the forest would get something to eat. The hunters could then count on the help of these little wood spirits to get more game.

When the meat was thoroughly smoked, it was packed into small bark barrels, often made on the spot. The hunters could then carry home some of the meat, as well as the skins of the game. The skins and meat were carefully hidden in the woods and picked up by the party on their way home. Now, loaded with spoils, the hunters moved more slowly. They often needed several weeks to complete their return journey home.

If a hunting party failed to return within the scheduled time, the families of the warriors became anxious about them. There was always a chance that they had been attacked while outside Iroquois territory. The women sent boys out along the trails to watch for the returning party. Sometimes a visitor to the village brought news of the men—news that was likely to be several weeks old—but it cheered the waiting families. When the returning party was sighted as it came slowly and heavily laden to the village, there was much rejoicing. Fires were kindled and pots set on the fires to boil in preparation for the coming feast. There was food for all and everyone had all he could eat. At feasts and festivals it was considered good manners to eat all you possibly could. This showed that you appreciated the food and the work of preparing it.

Perhaps even more exciting than the feast to the villagers were the stories that the returning hunters had to tell. They had been far away in a strange world and often among other tribes. The women and children and the old folks could hardly wait till the feast was over and the hunters had settled by the fires with their pipes. Then they would begin to tell about what they had seen and heard—meetings with other hunters in the great woods and their adventures in stalking the game they brought home.

After the first night was over, these stories were repeated again and again around the fires. Forgotten details were recalled, and at each retelling the audience listened closely for any changes. Such tales as these helped to pass the long winter evenings in the semidarkness of the longhouse.

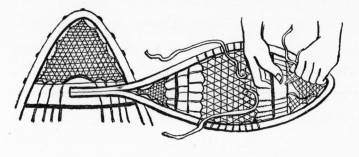

5

Winter

MANY OF the daily occupations of the Iroquois ended with winter and the coming of the
snow. The growing season was over. The harvest
was in. Some work continued outdoors, of course:
gathering firewood, hauling water, and hunting.
Hunting went on through most of the winter
except during storms. But the people spent a
good part of the winter months inside the longhouses.

When cold weather came, the women piled
firewood near their longhouses and stuffed dry
moss into the cracks between the sheets of bark

that formed the longhouse walls. New skins were hung over the doors, and each family mended and added more skins to the ones already hanging around their sleeping compartment. The heaviest clothes were worn all the time, for the longhouse was never warm and comfortable as our houses are today. The fires never heated the long drafty building. The earth floor was cold. The warmest place was close to the fire, so the families pulled their mats and fur robes as close to it as they could. They spread extra mats on the earth floor in an effort to keep warm.

Activities such as grinding corn and cooking, which were outdoor work in warm weather, were carried on near the fires. The longhouse became more crowded now that everyone was home and indoors. There was the constant noise of the pounding corn and there were always the strong smells of skins and cooking. But the Iroquois were used to the noise, the dimness, and the odors. Old men and women seldom left the longhouse during the winter. They kept busy doing their share of the work. Men spent hours and days slowly grinding a stone ax till the edge was smooth and sharp. Women cut the skins and, when there was enough light, sewed them into moccasins and shirts.

WOMAN SCRAPING SKIN

The cleaning and tanning of the skins had been done earlier when it was warmer. First they had been scraped and then soaked in a mixture of chopped oak and chestnut bark for tanning. Then the skins were stretched, dried, and rubbed with fat. After that they were smoked over a slow fire. This shrank and toughened the buckskin but left it as soft as ever. Tanned skins were stored away for finishing during the winter. The frozen skins of animals killed in the winter were piled outside the longhouse where they lay till spring, when they could be tanned.

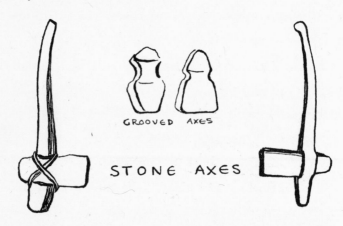

GROOVED AXES

STONE AXES

Men worked in the longhouse, too. Their work was not as exciting as the hunt or warpath, but it was important. Weapons were repaired. Bows were scraped and restrung. Drilling, flaking, and polishing stone tools were slow tasks that took days of labor. Men chipped and polished stone axheads. They bound these to wooden handles with wet rawhide which shrank as it dried and held the stone fast. Sometimes an axhead, polished during the winter, was set in the split stem of a hickory sapling early in the spring. As the hickory grew and the wood healed the wound, the stone axhead was locked tightly into place. A year or two later the sapling would be cut down and the ax would have a fine solid handle.

Bones from deer, bear, and smaller animals were saved and piled in a corner of the longhouse. During the winter they were split and polished to make awls, needles, harpoons, and arrowheads. Bear teeth were drilled and colored with red ocher. Gradually a necklace took form. It would be worn proudly at the next dance.

The making of snowshoes was men's work. Thin strips of ash wood were steamed over a pot of boiling water and bent into an oval shape until the two ends met. The ends were then pegged and tied together. Over this frame the men wove a net of rawhide thongs which shrank and tightened as they dried. The toe of the moccasin was fastened to the center of the snowshoe. The heel was left free.

Articles of wood were always used and always needed in the household. The men, especially the older men, carved bowls, ladles, and spoons. The work was done by the old method of burning and scraping away the charred wood. But the scraping

FLINT SCRAPER

MAN CARVING BOWL

FINISHED BOWLS

was done with great care on these small objects. Hour after hour the bowls and spoons were scraped with flint scrapers. Boys often helped the older men in this work. They copied and learned while they were helping.

If these occupations seem dull and uninteresting, that is exactly what they were. With few tools and fewer comforts, the Iroquois men and women spent many hours in slow hard work to meet the needs of daily life. It is no wonder that they were overwhelmed when explorers and later traders came with steel and copper, cloth and glass. Knives, axes, chisels, and other simple hand tools made it possible to finish a bowl, bow, or war club in a small fraction of the time it had taken before —and to do a better job, too. In the first century or so after they obtained these new tools, Iroquois men and women turned out handsome and artistic carvings, baskets, clothing, and other articles, all richly ornamented.

The Iroquois, like all people, suffered from minor ailments and injuries: upset stomachs, colds, headaches, toothaches, sprains, burns, and cuts. Accidents and illness were common in an Iroquois village. In winter, when people were cooped up inside the longhouse, there was more sickness than in summer. One reason for this was the lack of fresh food during the winter. Except for squash, there were no fresh vegetables at all and often no fresh meat. If the harvest had been poor, there might be famine before early summer brought new crops.

Every man and woman knew some simple remedies for illness and simple ways of treating injuries. But it was to the old women of the tribe that people turned when illness or injury needed special attention. In the summer and fall these women had gone to the fields and woods and had gathered roots, bark, and herbs. They had learned about these medicinal plants from their mothers and grandmothers. In turn, they taught the younger women about them.

The old women knew many kinds of remedies. They had teas and hot drinks for those who were ailing. Sassafras roots, slippery elm bark, and wild sarsaparilla were as well known to the Iroquois as aspirin and castor oil are to us. Oils and salves made of bear fat were applied to burns and bruises. Cuts and wounds were washed with warm water and bandaged with fresh cornhusks. The old women were respected because of this knowledge. Some even did a little surgery and knew how to set bones when they were broken.

Sometimes the remedies that the old women

used did not work. Perhaps the disease was serious. Perhaps the herbs were not the right cure. Then the patient took the next step. He tried to do something that would please and satisfy the spirits that had caused the sickness. Every Iroquois believed that evil spirits caused disease. These evil spirits, called Falsefaces, were horrible to look at. No one had ever seen one of these demons. If someone even came near a Falseface, it devoured itself as quick as a flash and disappeared. So the Iroquois believed.

To please the disease-bearing spirits, a secret society was organized in every village. No one in the village was supposed to know who its members were except the men who belonged to the society and one old woman who took care of the masks. This secret society was made up of men who had seen a spirit in a dream or who had been ill and believed they had been cured by the members of the society. When a man saw a spirit in a dream, he knew it was a summons that he could not ignore. He went to the old woman who kept the

Falseface masks and secretly told her his dream. She called the members of the society together, and at a feast the new member was added.

Members of the Falseface Society wore wooden masks when they appeared in ceremonies, and the first task of a new member was to make such a mask for himself. The man went alone to the woods and found a large basswood tree. He built a small fire near it and sprinkled some tobacco in the embers. Then he stripped off part of the bark and began to carve the mask in the living tree.

After the mask was outlined, he cut through the trunk of the tree above and below the mask. He split the log with the mask carved on it and carried the part with the mask to a bark shelter. The man remained in this shelter, where no one would see him, till his mask was carved and polished. The white wood was rubbed with charcoal or red ocher to color it. Grease made it smooth and shiny. When the Iroquois had metal, eyes of brass made the mask more frightening.

So if the simple teas and other remedies failed to cure an illness or if the patient requested it, the Falseface Society was invited to come and help. The masked warriors entered the house of the sick person in single file, stepping in rhythm and shaking their turtle-shell rattles. One man was invited to sing for them. Each Falseface dancer stopped as he passed the fire and scooped up some ashes. These he blew on the head of the sick person. They danced around and around him. Toward the end of the dance, the sick person often joined them. If he was unable to walk, one of the dancers carried him. As the dancers left the longhouse, they received gifts of food and tobacco from the patient's family. The dancing and singing were supposed to please the Falseface spirits, who would then depart from the longhouse.

1. TURTLE   2. GOURD

RATTLES

Sickness in the village sometimes brought death. When an old man died, the body was dressed in the best buckskins and placed on a bark scaffold outside the village. The man's bow and arrows, war club, and a pouch containing parched corn and dried meat were set beside him. On a dead woman's scaffold the relatives placed her sewing awl, her husking awl, her burden basket with its embroidered tumpline, and some food. The Iroquois believed that a person who died had to make a long

journey westward to the land of the spirits. He would need tools and food for this journey.

Months later the bones of the dead were put in a small bark house near the family's longhouse. There the bones of all the other dead relatives were kept. When a village moved, a large grave was dug and all these bones were buried together.

A year after a person's death, his relatives held a mourning ceremony. But this mourning ceremony was a joyful one. The relatives believed that the dead warrior had at last reached the end of the long journey. He would live now in peace and comfort, leading a life very much like that of the people below. A hunter would find plenty of game to hunt and a woman would have the finest buckskin for making clothing. In the land of the spirits, a boy who died would grow up to become as good a hunter and warrior as he would have been on earth. A girl would work in fields where the crops would always be plentiful.

As winter reached its peak and the days began to grow longer, the people looked forward to the

Midwinter Festival which would break the routine of winter living. This was the longest of all Iroquois festivals. It was celebrated for a whole week beginning late in January or early in February, and everyone took part. Hunters hurried home to be in time for the festivities. Boys looked forward to it especially, because it was a time, like our Halloween, when they could get into mischief without being scolded.

The village council decided on the day when the Midwinter Festival was to begin, and messengers were sent around to announce the decision to the people. Preparations began at once. Longhouses were put in order; the dirt floors were swept clean. The village grounds were tidied. Ashes and rubbish were removed, and firewood was piled neatly near the longhouses. The best clothing was made ready.

On the morning of the first day, young and old put on their best garments and sat by the longhouse fires talking and waiting. Soon two messengers, dressed in bearskins with cornhusk wreaths around their heads, arms, and legs, knocked on the door. On entering the longhouse they announced: "Listen, listen, listen! The ceremonies which the Great Spirit has commanded us to perform are about to begin." They chanted

a song and left to go from longhouse to longhouse with the same message. In the afternoon, the messengers came again to tell everyone the festival was under way.

The Midwinter Festival was a religious one.

The Iroquois enjoyed it, but they kept the important things of the festival constantly in mind. Because all things white were sacred to the Great Spirit, a white dog was strangled on the first day of the festival as a sacrifice. The dead dog was then spotted with red paint and people came forward with ornaments and necklaces to decorate its body.

On the following day people went from longhouse to longhouse. At each one they asked the families sitting by their fires to guess what they had dreamed. Sometimes they carried a tool or object to give a clue. A woman might carry a digging stick because she had dreamed of cultivating corn and getting a fine harvest. If the dream had to do with the future, and if anyone guessed what it was, the dreamer tried his best to live up to his dream in the days ahead.

While this was going on, the messengers of the first day, now dressed and painted as warriors with feathers in their hair, visited each family three times a day. With wooden shovels they sprinkled ashes from the fires around the room, saying: "I thank the Great Spirit that he has spared our lives again to witness this New Year's celebration." All joined in a thanksgiving song and the messengers moved on to another house.

Small parties of dancers went from longhouse to longhouse where the people, still dressed in their best clothes, waited for them. Each group had a leader, supplied its own music, and did a special dance. One group did the feather dance, another the trotting dance, still another the fish dance. Older boys, dressed as warriors, came around dancing the war dance with loud war whoops. Following them came other boys in old torn buckskins, wearing masks. With them was an old woman with a huge basket. If these beggars were welcomed and given presents, they put their gifts in the basket, did a dance to show their thanks, and departed. But if the presents were not enough, the boys scattered around and grabbed whatever they could lay their hands on. If they were caught, they returned what they had taken; but if they escaped with the loot, it was their prize.

Next day all the articles that had been seized were set out for the people to see. The owners could ransom them by paying what they were worth in food. With all the gifts and ransoms the boys had a feast.

The sixth and seventh days of the Midwinter Festival were devoted to games. A favorite with the boys at this time was playing with snow-snakes. A snow-snake was a slender, carefully carved hickory stick, five to seven feet long and about half an inch thick. The boys dragged a heavy log through the snow, making a long straight groove. The weight of the log packed the snow hard. Standing at one end, the boys took turns hurling their snake down the groove with an underhand throw. The boy who threw the snake farthest was the winner.

Indoors the warriors and the older men played the cherry-stone or bowl game. A large crowd stood around watching, for this was a gambling game and the stakes were always high. All kinds of personal possessions were used for bets and were placed with the two umpires in charge of the game. The cherry stones were colored black on one side and white on the other. The men took turns rolling them in a   oden bowl. If five out of the six cherry stones showed the same color when the bowl was set down, the man who shook it won one point. If all six stones showed the same color, that counted five points. Men took turns till one team had won a hundred points.

By the time the Midwinter Festival was over, every Iroquois felt that the winter's backbone had been broken. Even though there were long cold days ahead, the people did not mind the weather so much. They began to work at repairing snow-shoes, troughs, and utensils for making maple syrup. The smell of spring was in the air.

There was one bright side to much of the winter work in the longhouse. Families sat around the fires chatting and laughing as they worked. Men and boys told jokes and talked of the hunt, while the women and girls listened. The boys played war games and the little girls were

busy playing house. Everyone enjoyed being together. The older boys edged over near the warriors and tried to imitate their speech and man-
ner. There were arguments, too, and when they
got out of hand it was a grandmother who told
both sides to quiet down, and they did.

The best times in the longhouse were those
winter evenings when the old men talked. The
Iroquois men were great storytellers. The tribes
had no way of writing down their songs and stories.
So they were memorized and repeated over and
over again. The old men who knew the stories best

told many of them at these winter gatherings. When the young men grew up, they told the same 'stories to their own children. From these stories the children learned the history and legends of their people.

The Iroquois considered it most important that a story be told or a song sung exactly as it had been heard. This may seem impossible to us who are so used to reading from a book. But the Iroquois listened so carefully and had such good memories that they could repeat a long story or chant without a mistake.

These winter stories were unlike those told by hunters. Hunters told tales of personal adventure. Such stories belonged to the warrior who told them and only the owner of a story could tell it in public. The stories the old men told were legends that belonged to all the people. But the rules as to when and how they could be told were very strict. These strict rules made these legends of great deeds and powerful magic, performed by men and animals, all the more interesting to the listeners, who believed every word was true.

The legends could not be told during the summer. If they were, people would gather to listen and would neglect the fields and the hunt. Children would go hungry and older people would grow lazy and shiftless. So the tales could only be told in winter when the harvests were all in. They could never be told outdoors. If they were, birds and other animals might hear and be offended, because in the stories men often outwitted the animals. There was also the chance that animals might learn from the stories and become too smart for the hunters. So legends could only be told inside the longhouse. If anyone broke these rules, the little wood spirits would send wasps to sting the storyteller's tongue and lips. A snake would crawl into his bed at night and choke him. The rules, therefore, were strictly obeyed.

When a storyteller was about to begin, he motioned to the people in the longhouse to gather closely around. "*Hanio, hanio,*" he called. "Get ready. I am about to begin."

As the tale was told, the people interrupted to exclaim, "Hah, hah," so the storyteller would know that everyone approved. If the listeners failed to say "Hah" often enough, the storyteller stopped. Perhaps they did not like the story.

When a listener wanted to move away from the circle, he said, "*Siganah,*" which meant "Please tie the story." The storyteller then stopped and everyone waited till the person returned. If a person fell asleep during the story, everyone was angry with him. Then the storyteller was bound to start the story over again from the beginning. It had not been properly tied when the person fell asleep. When a storyteller stopped talking, he always said *"Daneho"*—"That's the end."

If you had been in a Seneca longhouse on a winter's night, you might have heard an old man's voice calling, *"Hanio, hanio."* Then, as you sat by the fire with all the others, you would have heard the story of the man-eating wife.

"Once, long ago, a man, his wife, and their dog, who was old and faithful, lived by themselves in a clearing in the forest. The man hunted. The woman kept house and worked in the cornfield. One day when the woman sat by the fire baking corn bread in the ashes, a spark burned her finger. It began to blister. So she licked it with her tongue and then put the finger in her mouth. In this way she got a taste of her own burned finger—and she liked the taste.

"The woman took a flint knife, cut off the burned flesh from her finger, and ate it. It tasted so good that she grabbed a glowing ember, burned another place on her arm, cut off the flesh, and ate that. She enjoyed this very much, so she kept burning and eating herself till she had eaten all the flesh she could reach on her arms and legs. Then she picked up a stick, pushed the marrow out of her bones, and ate it too. She filled her hollow bones with pebbles, and the pebbles rattled as she moved. 'That sounds good,' she exclaimed, pausing every now and then in her eating to dance a little and listen to the rattling in her legs and arms. 'That sounds very, very good!'

"The dog sat by the fire and watched the woman. When she finished eating the marrow from her bones, she said to him, 'You had better run and find your master and tell him to get away and take you with him. If he doesn't, I'll eat you both.'

"The old faithful dog ran as fast as he could, and when he came to where his master was hunting he told him what had happened and how his wife had become a man-eater. The man and the dog both started to run, but the dog was old and his legs were short. He could not run fast enough. So the man put him into a hollow tree and ordered him to turn to wood. The dog was willing to do this because he wanted his master to save himself. Then the man ran on alone as fast as he could, till he came to a river with high banks. An old man sat by the river.

" 'Help me, Grandfather,' the man cried, 'I'm in great trouble. My wife is following me. She wants to kill and eat me. Help me. Put me across the river.'

" 'I know she is following you,' said the old man calmly. 'But she is still a long way off. I will put you across the river, but first you must bring me a basketful of fish from my fish pond.'

"By the side of the pond was a basket and a dip net. The man dipped the net into the water and caught many fish. He filled the basket and carried it back to the old man. 'Sit down and eat with me,' the old man said after he had cooked the fish. They ate together. 'Now bring me a basketful of groundnuts,' the old man ordered.

As fast as he could, the man dug up the ground-nuts in the old man's garden and brought them over to the fire. After he had cooked and eaten the nuts, the old man said, 'Now I will put you across the river.'

"The old man lay down on the river bank and, leaning on his elbows, stretched his neck right across the river to the opposite bank. 'Walk across my neck,' he said, 'but be careful. I am not as strong as I used to be.'

"The man walked across carefully and thanked the old man.

"In the meantime, the man-eating wife had started off after her husband. She soon came upon his tracks and followed him. Every now and then she stopped to dance and listen with delight to the rattling in her bones. Then she went on again. When she came to the river and saw the old man, she screamed at him, 'Old man, come and put me across the river. I am following my husband. I'm hungry. Be quick.'

"But the old man was not to be hurried. 'I can't put you across,' he said. 'I don't want to help a woman who is chasing her husband to eat him up!'

"The woman begged and argued till at last the old man said, 'I'll put you across, but first you must bring me a basketful of fish and dig me a basketful of groundnuts in my garden.' The woman brought the fish and nuts, but would not eat with the old man after he had cooked the food. She said she wanted to eat only human flesh.

"After he finished eating, the old man went over to the edge of the river bank. He stretched his neck across the river. This time, however, he arched and curved it like a deer's antlers. The woman became angry. 'I can't walk on that,' she she screamed. 'I'll fall in.'

" 'You can do as you like,' said the old man. 'I am old. I can't make my neck flat any more. It would break. You must walk very carefully.'

"The woman continued to scold, but she had no choice. She could either stay where she was and be hungry or cross the river on the arched neck. At last she started, carefully picking her steps and scolding as she went. The river was deep and full of terrible creatures. When she reached the middle of the river, the old man, angry with her scolding, jerked his neck. The man-eating wife fell into the water and the creatures there seized and devoured her.

"After traveling for several days, the hunter came to a village and met a lovely maiden whom he married, and they lived happily ever after.

"*Daneho!*"

6

The Iroquois Today

To SPEAK of the Iroquois entirely in the past is not right. A good many of them still live among us. In the early 1600's there were about fifteen thousand Iroquois living in about twenty villages. Today there are still almost as many Iroquois, living mostly in New York State and nearby Canada. Some have moved into Wisconsin and Oklahoma. Although the number of Iroquois now and hun-

dreds of years ago is about the same, great changes
have taken place. The tribes which were once
the most powerful in the East are now almost
forgotten in a world full of so many new things.
Cities have grown where villages and camp sites
once stood. Cement highways follow many of the
old Iroquois trails across New York State, because
these trails long ago set the easiest routes.

Events that happened during the years when
the first Europeans came to this part of North
America set a pattern for the two centuries
that followed.

There was, for example, the meeting of the
Iroquois with the first European they had ever
seen—Samuel de Champlain. Champlain was a
French explorer who came to Canada by way of
the St. Lawrence River. From there, in 1609, he
came down the lake that now bears his name with
a party of Huron warriors. The Hurons were old
enemies of the Iroquois. Champlain made friends
with the Hurons and, therefore, had to promise to
help them against the Iroquois. When a party of

Hurons went to raid an Iroquois camp near the spot that is now Fort Ticonderoga, Champlain joined his friends, the Hurons. The warriors on both sides lined up for battle. But before a single war whoop sounded, the ranks of the Hurons parted and out stepped Champlain, dressed in shining armor and holding a strange weapon. Champlain fired two shots at the staring Mohawks and two Mohawk warriors fell dead, despite their wooden armor. The Iroquois turned and ran and the Hurons followed and defeated them.

Soon the Iroquois learned the mystery of firearms and obtained them from the traders. They were so delighted with these new weapons that they could not shoot their flintlocks often enough. They used up all their powder shooting at trees, at their dogs, and even at each other, just to see how the guns worked. It was some time before this curiosity wore off. Besides getting guns, the Iroquois also obtained metal and tools, axes and tomahawks from the traders.

The Dutch, French, and later the English

traders were anxious to buy furs from the Iroquois, particularly beaver pelts. Since the territory of the Iroquois connected with the rich fur regions to the northwest, the traders wanted to make friends with the Iroquois. They induced the Iroquois to get furs for them from other Indian tribes. The Iroquois warriors enjoyed trading so much that soon some of them gave up hunting altogether. They became fur traders. These fur traders traveled for hundreds of miles inland and bartered tomahawks, metal knives, and cloth for furs.

With their improved weapons and the friendship of the Europeans, the Iroquois could force neighboring tribes into submission. Some of these tribes gave up quickly, no doubt frightened of the Iroquois firearms, as the Iroquois had once been of the French. Others had to be conquered in long wars. By 1650, as the Europeans gained control of all the land along the coast, the Iroquois had gained control of all the inland territory east of the Mississippi River as far south as Virginia and northern Tennessee. Settlers from the Five Nations were scattered throughout their new territory to watch over the conquered tribes and maintain peace. The conquered tribes paid the Iroquois tribute in furs and food.

The warriors of these conquered tribes were forbidden to go on the warpath. This shamed them, for a man who cannot fight is no better than a woman. In the north, the Huron victory over the Iroquois could now be avenged. The Iroquois returned to Huron territory, armed and in large numbers. The Hurons could not retreat fast enough and soon nearly all were killed, even though the French had given them firearms, too.

But all these victories had their price. Many Iroquois warriors—the youngest and strongest men in the tribes—had died. Fields had been neglected and the villages needed repairs. From 1650 to about 1685 the mighty League of the Five Nations was at peace. Longhouses were repaired. Fresh cornfields were cleared and planted in the old as well as the new Iroquois territories.

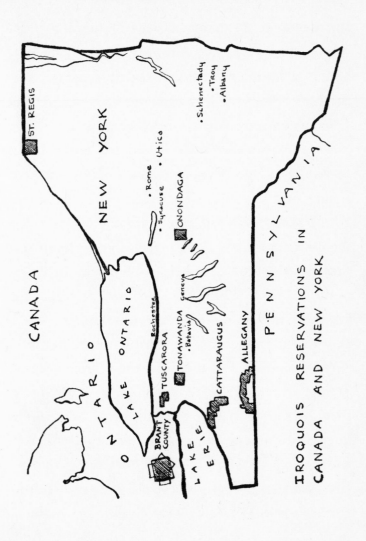

IROQUOIS RESERVATIONS IN CANADA AND NEW YORK

Many captives were adopted into the tribes to replace dead warriors. This was a time of activity and plenty. Trade with the Dutch and the French continued. In 1664 the English began their long friendship with the Iroquois.

Beyond the Iroquois borders European colonies were spreading. In 1715 the Tuscarora Indians, who were related to the Iroquois, were pushed out of their lands in North Carolina. Refugees began to flee into Iroquois territory and appealed to the Five Nations for help. The League accepted the Tuscarora and gave the refugees some land in Oneida territory. Later the Tuscarora were invited into the Council of the Five Nations but were given no vote. However, the Council was known as the Council of the Six Nations after that.

Even at this early time, the Iroquois way of life was beginning to change. In some ways their life was easier. Now they had metal tools and woven cloth. Other conveniences came soon after. It was not long before the Iroquois began to abandon their longhouses and build log cabins, made possible by the ax and the saw. This split them up into smaller family groups. But the feeling of kinship, which was so important in the long-house, did not weaken.

Missionaries had followed soon after the ex-plorers. The French tried to win Iroquois friend-ship through their missionaries. The French mis-sionaries were the first to come to work among the Iroquois. They opened schools for the chil-dren and began to teach the Iroquois better farm-ing methods. They brought plows; they tried to teach about preserving food and the use of farm animals. These French missionaries made many converts among the Mohawk and Onondaga. But these converts were regarded by the other Iro-quois as traitors.

Later, about 1750, Anglican missionaries came into Iroquois territory. Because of the Iroquois friendship with the English, these missionaries were somewhat more popular than the French. They too built schoolhouses and worked in the

villages. They translated parts of the Bible into
the Iroquois languages. All these changes, working through two or three generations, took the
Iroquois people away from their old customs and
made their lives very different.

There was trouble between the French and the
English, which grew sharper year by year, leading
to wars. These bitter wars between the English
and the French were for the possession of the
rich lands in the northeast. From 1755 to 1763
the Iroquois were involved in these wars, now
known as the French and Indian Wars. Most Iroquois fought on the side of the English, but the
Mohawk and Onondaga converts fought with the
French against their own people.

The peace that followed the English victory
over the French did not last long. Soon trouble
between the American colonists and the English
grew serious. In 1775 it flared up into war. Both
sides sent delegates to the Council of the Six
Nations. The American delegates said: "This is a
family quarrel between us and old England. You

Indians are not concerned in it. Remain at home. Do not join either side." The Oneida chiefs agreed to this. "Let us remain neutral," they pleaded before the Council. "After the war, we will make a treaty with the victors."

But the Iroquois respected friendship. Joseph Brant, a Mohawk chief, who had been called the "Great Captain of the Six Nations," said to the Council: "I have learned to live as a good subject of the English and to honor the king. A Mohawk must remain true to his beliefs. He cannot change them." Brant was ready to lead his warriors against the colonists.

Since the rules of the League required that all the chiefs agree to each decision of the Council, the stand of the Oneidas kept the Iroquois from joining the British, even though the majority wanted to. But the League had already been weakened, and it was finally agreed to let each tribe act for itself. The Oneidas and with them about half of the Tuscarora warriors remained neutral. The Seneca, Mohawk, Cayuga, Onondaga, and the remaining Tuscarora fought against the American colonists. Thus the League itself was the first victim of the Revolutionary War.

As the war got under way in 1777, the Iroquois under Joseph Brant gathered at Oswego and at Niagara. Altogether about fifteen hundred of them served with the British army. They drove out settlers who were not loyal to the British and then joined St. Leger, a British general. A battle was fought at Oriskany in eastern New York. It was the first of many in which the Iroquois took part. Settlements between the Hudson River and the Great Lakes were no longer safe. A number of them were wiped out by Indian raids. In revenge, colonial troops went through the Iroquois lands, burning cabins and villages, cornfields and forests. Famine and disease killed hundreds of Iroquois, who were left starving in winter.

Peace was made in 1783. But the British did little to take care of the Iroquois who had helped them, beyond giving them a large tract of land on both sides of the Grand River in Ontario.

Many Mohawk and Cayuga moved into Canada.

Some colonists wanted to drive the Iroquois out of the country, but George Washington was against this. To this day the Iroquois gratefully recall how George Washington stood up for them. They even say that although only Iroquois can enter the Iroquois heaven, George Washington is one exception because he was kind to the People of the Longhouse.

In 1784, a treaty with the Iroquois was signed at Fort Stanwix in Rome, New York. In this agreement the Iroquois gave up all the land they had conquered in the past century, retaining only the land that was originally theirs in central New York. But this treaty brought no peace. The British at Niagara and Detroit still stirred the Iroquois against the united colonists, and it was not until ten years later that peace was established. Several later treaties set up reservations for the Iroquois tribes.

The Iroquois believed that the land had been given by the Creator to their ancestors. They believed it could be used and might even be conquered. But land could not be traded or sold like corn or furs. So at Fort Stanwix the Iroquois chiefs could not understand the idea of giving up their land. They did not own the land and could not honestly sign it away. The Americans, on the other hand, could not understand the Iroquois point of view. Finally, the defeated Iroquois gave in. Once the land started to go, it went faster and faster. New York State and many private land agents bargained for and bought land from the chiefs.

In the early 1800's the Iroquois had to start all over again, clearing woodlands on their reservations. They lacked man power and money for tools. The League still existed, but separate treaties with the colonists had been made by the different tribal chiefs without permission from the League. Red Jacket, a Seneca, had tried to prevent this, but without success. These were, indeed, bad times for the Iroquois.

It was then, when things were at their worst,

that another Seneca, Handsome Lake, began traveling among the tribes, telling them stories about his visions and urging the Iroquois to go back to their old way of life. Handsome Lake

HANDSOME   LAKE

preached that they must give up their new beliefs and stop despairing. Liquor had caused trouble among the Iroquois. Handsome Lake preached against its use. Many Iroquois saw hope in the teachings of this leader and were ready to follow him. The work of Handsome Lake helped the Iroquois but it also divided them. Those who did not believe in his teachings were unfriendly to those who did. When Handsome Lake died on

NEWTOWN LONGHOUSE
CATTARAUGUS RESERVATION

the Onondaga Reservation in 1815, he had a large following. Many Iroquois in New York and Canada still follow his teachings today.

It took another century for the land and treaty problems of the Iroquois to be settled. Now about half of these people live in New York State and about half live in Canada, on seven reservations. Schools have been established on the reservations and the land has been improved. Iroquois now follow trades of all kinds. Many are farmers and mechanics. Others go to college and become teachers, doctors, and businessmen. One group of Mohawks has found unusual work. They are steel construction men who build high bridges, towers, and skyscrapers. Gangs of Mohawk construction men have worked on almost every famous bridge and skyscraper in the United States and Canada. They have no fear of high places and like this exciting work.

On the reservations the Iroquois live in simple frame houses and cottages. Some still live in log cabins. Each reservation has a longhouse built of

modern materials where the tribe meets for ceremonies and festivals. Many of the old festivals
are still observed and enjoyed. The Green Corn
Festival and the Midwinter Festival are times of
feasting and fun. Some of the older men carve
masks and the women make cornhusk dolls. The
older boys play baseball and football, but lacrosse
is still a favorite game and snow-snakes appear
in winter. A State Fair is held at Syracuse, New
York, every fall. Onondaga from the nearby reservation come there to sell sweet-grass baskets and
other souvenirs. Many of the descendants of the
Iroquois who settled along the Grand River in
Canada now own prosperous farms with modern
equipment.

Today Iroquois children go to school with
the other children who live near them. They all
speak English as well as their own tongues. The
boys are often the best athletes and runners in the
school. The League still exists and every Iroquois
child is told the history of his people. The Iroquois still consider themselves a nation. Not so

long ago the League appointed the Museum of
the State of New York as keeper of its wampum,
and there in Albany you can see the famous Iroquois wampum belts, records of a glorious past.

Index

* Indicates illustrations.

157